Dedicated to the memory of my comrade and friend,
J. KEIR HARDIE,
whose inspired wisdom and faith, unwearying toil, and noble courage and
patience, did so much to lead the working class forth on the road to socialism.

J. BRUCE GLASIER

Socialism and Strikes J. Bruce Glasier
First Prism Key Press Edition 2012

Prism Key Press
New York, NY 10001
PrismKeyPress.com

ISBN-13: 978-1468139525

Socialism and Strikes
J. Bruce Glasier

CONTENTS

Preface and Apologia

THIS pamphlet was first published some twenty-five years ago, under the title of **On Strikes**; it had a large circulation , but has been for many years out of print, and I have been urged to have it reprinted.

This I was at first reluctant to do, as I thought I should have to revise and perhaps re-write a large portion of it in order to bring the statement up to date with the changed circumstances of the industrial and political world. But on reading over the pamphlet after twenty or more years, I am almost startled to find how appropriate for the most part the paragraphs remain to the present situation in the Trade Union and Socialist Movements. Except for an occasional mode of expression and a few topical references, I observe little in its pages that I should change were I to write it afresh today. I am therefore allowing the pamphlet to go forth almost exactly as it was originally written, except that in one or two places I have altered a phrase or substituted fresh references to wage figures and passing events.

The stupendous events of the revolutionary upheavals in Eussia and Central Europe, and the enormously augmented power of mass-action now possessed by Trade Unions in our own country, have not rendered obsolete the main pleas in the pamphlet with respect to the present situation. Eather have they served to demonstrate the wisdom and urgency more than ever of the great political mission which the Socialist movement set forth to accomplish. That mission was avowedly to organise the workers for political action, in order to bring not only the claims of Labour, but all questions affecting the common wellbeing, before the judgment of the whole people.

The extraordinary spectacle which, were it not so appallingly serious and tragic, would be so grotesquely

7

ludicrous, of the workers penalising themselves and the poor everywhere by directing virtually the six million-fold power of Labour to the antediluvian device of seeking to overcome the power of capitalism by an incessant effort to force up wages to meet an incessant rise in prices, justifies the hope that a reaffirmation of the arguments contained in the pamphlet may be of real advantage at the present hour.

No one will, I hope, so misread the pamphlet as to suppose that it countenances for a moment the notion that the workers should relinquish the strike as an industrial or even as a political weapon. I cannot conceive of the workers ever surrendering the right to collectively withhold their labour in industrial bargaining or in certain political eventualities under a Capitalist, and even under a Socialist regime.

What the sort of eventualities are that make justifiable the recourse to strike action will always depend on the nature of the principle at stake and the state of intelligence, discipline and political capacity of the workers concerned. But in a country possessing complete political freedom – and especially where the workers are in such numbers as to be able to make or unmake Governments and laws – the mass strike should be used only as a last resource, when the will of the people is being overborne by unconstitutional action on the part of the Government – by military or police intimidation, or by sectional usurpation of public power. For the mass strike puts the whole community, and chiefly the poor, under penalty, and only in such extreme instances as I have suggested can the workers fairly and in accord with the mutual obligations of human society resort to what is virtually a form of civil war.

Let us not forget that revolutionism and mass-action, strikes and dictatorships are old: many a thousand years older than parliaments and the universal franchise. It was but yesterday that women and the whole adult working class obtained the vote: and as yet the half of them hardly have any notion of the purpose and power of their new-found citizenship.

8

My argument, then, is frankly an appeal from the strike to the ballot-box, from hunger and fear and terrorism of all kind, to reason, to the true self-interest and the inherent goodwill of the community of the nation. For if there be not enough reason and sense of common well-being and inherent goodwill in the community to bring about Socialism, how can we hope that there will be enough to keep Socialism going after it has been established by terror and force? Terror and force do not breed reason and goodwill. Nay, a Socialism established by terror and intimidation would be no Socialism at all.

Political democracy has not failed: it has never yet been really tried. War, rebellion, and all forms of terrorism, compulsion, repression and punishment, these have been tried from the beginning, and behold, the world we see!

J. Bruce Glasier
May 1920

Chapter I

AMONG the many curious and, at first sight, inexplicable customs of modern civilisation, that of industrial strikes seems one of the most extraordinary. Even writing, as I do, in the heart of a district where 75,000 men are in the seventh week of a contest of this kind, I find difficulty in convincing myself that such a thing as a strike, especially on a large scale, is a probable or even possible occurrence.

It seems almost beyond belief that a method so irrational and futile of determining questions of right dealing between man and man should be resorted to by an intelligent, practical, and, shall I say, religious community.

An actual fight with fists, swords, or guns, in which men deal ponderable blows of some sort, one can understand – it may at least determine a question of might, if not of right; but a contest between two parties as to which shall do nothing and, maybe, eat nothing, longest, with a view to deciding a question of either might or right, seems ridiculous beyond the reach of words.

Nevertheless, strikes are not only a fact of our time, but they are regarded by many people, especially amongst the working class, as being quite as natural and inevitable occurrences as thunderstorms, blizzards, earthquakes and other physical disturbances that usually play havoc with human life and property. And the more terrible their effects – the more the sufferings of women and children can be cited and the patience of the men commended – the more justifiable they are esteemed.

Strikes are especially frequent in Christian countries, although upon what particular passage of Scripture their authorisation rests I am unable to say. They occur most regularly in those districts where large and handsome churches have been erected through the beneficence of rich employers of labour and their devout daughters. Whenever you see a church being built you may rest assured that there will be a strike in the neighbourhood before the copper weathercock is perched upon the spire. New churches are decidedly unlucky in this respect, and should always be regarded with grave suspicion by the working classes. It is significant that, whereas clergymen in their prayers confidently communicate to the Almighty their desire for the success of British troops in battles abroad, they seldom venture a word of supplication on behalf of British armies of Labour on strike at home.

Although no actual fighting usually takes place in the course of a strike, the struggle is frequently as brutal in its intent and as devastating in its effect as a military engagement. Most of the vices and but few of the virtues that are supposed to be attached to war on the field are exemplified. All the magnificent exertion and adventure, and the heroic comradeship which of ten time characterise campaigning on the field, are usually absent; and weary, blunting idleness, and mean suspicion, hatred, and deception are encouraged instead. Women and children rather than the men themselves have to bear the heaviest load of suffering; and the harm to their bodies inflicted by, it may be, months of continuous privation, and in the winter time of torturing cold, is often such that almost as much wreck and ruin is done to human life as would occur were a similar number of men employed in a war of rival nations.

And, indeed, so far as strikes can be dignified by the name of war, they are wars between rival nations – not nations in the sense of people belonging to different countries, but of people having different interests, habits and obligations – the nation of the rich and idle and the nation of the poor and industrious. And, if you look at it closely, you will find that the cause of strikes is precisely the same as the cause of wars. Usually when one country seeks to invade another it does so with the object of appropriating the land and riches of the other nation and subjecting its people to some form of servitude. It is precisely with this object that employers seek to reduce their workmen's wages or oppose trade unions, thereby provoking the workmen to strike. The employers – by which term I wish to include the land and capital-owning classes – desire to obtain more riches and idleness for themselves by appropriating a still further portion of their workmen's wages or leisure. The workmen endeavour to resist this, just as one nation resists invasion by another; but, as I think we shall see later on, their method of resistance is of very little effect, and even when they seem to have gained a victory it is only for the moment, and at best they have only compelled the employers to be content with a little less plunder than they otherwise would have secured.

In strikes as in wars, therefore, justice has no say in the issue of the conflict – might is right; victory is vindication. The factory becomes a fortress in a state of siege. The workmen wish to get into it to be employed under the terms of their union; the employer refuses to allow them save on his own terms, and bribes other workmen – blacklegs – to occupy their vacated posts, hoping that destitution will ere long compel the rebellious trade unionists to offer submission to his rule and crave back employment on his conditions. The strikers endeavour to intercept the blacklegs from garrisoning the employer's place, and also hope to compel him to surrender by jeopardising his custom and destroying his profits. Whichever side can hold out the longest wins. But, as I have said before, although it has the semblance of a fight, it is little better than a starvation contest, and chiefly interesting as an experiment in physiological and economic endurance. By the rules of the engagement neither side is supposed to touch the person or property of the other. The workmen merely set themselves to scare the employer into yielding through fear of incurring greater loss by holding out than by giving in, while the employer deliberately, and with the approval of his own and the public conscience, prays Famine to do service for him, well knowing that the men will stick out only so long as their ribs stick in. It is all very droll and very ghastly.

Great, moreover, as are the number of workmen effected in many instances, and momentous as may be the issues involved, strikes are nevertheless usually deadly dull affairs. Nobody is ever really enthusiastic about them, and although the newspapers occasionally contain long accounts of the very great ones, everybody forgets all about them as soon as they are settled and never wish to be reminded of them again. You never see boys poring over the pages of a Trades Union newspaper, and no enterprising publisher has ever thought of issuing a popular companion volume to **British Battles on Land and Sea**, entitled, **Strikes and Lock-outs from the Thames to the Tay**.

People will rush in thousands to see a football match or a couple of drunken men fight, but during even the greatest strikes hardly a soul will think of wandering down to the scene of the dispute unless a riot between the strikers and blacklegs is expected. And here I may opportunely remark how much more valiantly workmen comport themselves towards poor starving blacklegs than towards the fat and comfortable employers who hire these unfortunate wretches. Scores of blacklegs have been mauled in the course of strikes, but scarcely so much as one employer has had even his whiskers singed.

The reason of the indifference of the public towards strikes is not far to seek. People know that a strike is an irrational and foolish affair, and that there is no real go in it. They don't like to see men knocking about hungry, with their women and children starving at home, and they cannot be persuaded that there is any right reason for such a proceeding. If the workmen, not knowing better what to do, even said: "Our masters refuse to pay us what we are entitled to, and unless we consent to be robbed by them we must stop work and begin to starve; let us therefore seize our masters as we would any other sneak-thieves and duck them in the river, and then let us go to our municipal councils, and if they refuse to give us work, let us duck them too" – then you would see the situation brightening. People would believe there was some earnestness in the matter, and crowds of interested and, I venture to say, approving spectators would flock to the scene. But for men to allege that they are being swindled, and endeavour to show how deeply they feel the injustice of it by going in for a few weeks' starvation is in no wise an exhilarating event. And thus it is that strikes, notwithstanding the tragedy and magnificence of resolution which is often attached to them, are reckoned about as uninteresting as funerals.

We cannot dissociate the unreality of carrying on strikes from the motive that urges men to declare them. Most commonly the professed object is to obtain a rise or resist a reduction of wages. In other words, as I have already observed, the men insinuate that their master is intent upon, or has already succeeded in, cheating them out of their due. But although the fact of the case is usually as clear as day, it is perfectly evident that in most instances the workmen are not quite sure about it, and are not without a lurking suspicion that, after all, it may be they themselves and not their master who are endeavouring to do the cheating. For, did you ever know of a workman who really believed he was being defrauded of money behaving as workmen do when on strike?

I remember once observing the behaviour of a workman who really thought his master designed to cheat him. He was a moulder, and the dispute was all over the paltry sum of twopence, which he held had been knavishly deducted from his pay. In three minutes the pay-box was the scene of what appeared to be an incipient riot. All the dynamic expletives usually excluded from publication were exploding on the premises. The cashier was brought down, then the manager, and finally two policemen had to be summoned to give *éclat* to the proceedings. It was a splendid scene. There stood the little black moulder, the great streaks of sweat dripping down upon his indigo shirt, and his clenched fist in ugly proximity with the cashier's nose, threatening to bring it down as a preliminary to calling in the entire forces of the Crown and Constitution to vindicate his right should the twopence not be restored to him

15

on the spot!

That, I say, is an example of real trenchant indignation displayed by a single workman against what he firmly believed was an attempt to defraud him of twopence. Fancy, then, what ten thousand or a hundred thousand men, imbued with the same private pluck and public spirit, would do if they all conceived themselves to be robbed, not of a couple of coppers once perhaps in a lifetime, but of so many shillings every week? Multiply even that one man's unit of protestation against being fleeced of twopence by the square of a hundred thousand men – why, it would shake the foundations of the empire and bring the whole fabric of the State rattling down about our ears!

And yet, when over 300,000 English miners were on strike in 1893 for nearly five months, and although they were resisting an attempt on the part of their employers to defraud each of them of five shillings a week, not once did their demeanour give occasion for political alarm, never once did they threaten the stability of the social edifice. Indeed, the only incendiary or insurrectionary incident that disturbed the Sabbath-peace of the combatants was occasioned as usual by those who are paid and appointed to preserve it. At Featherstone some soldiers, mistaking, no doubt, a peaceful assembly of black-faced miners for a tribe of Arabs or Hottentots, poured a volley of Lee-Metford bullets into their midst. For months the newspapers recorded with gruesome minuteness the heart-rending scenes of destitution among the miners' families. Subscriptions were raised for them, philanthropists flecked to the front, and politicians – as is their wont on such occasions – beat unobtrusively in the background. Towards the latter days of the dispute, when the weather became bitterly cold, hundreds of thousands of poor people who were in no wise responsible for the strike endured appalling misery from the coal famine. And this was, up to that time, the greatest strike ever known in England! In what respect, save in increased magnitude of the numbers of the strikers and in the wider infliction of suffering upon the community generally, with perhaps a compensating shortening of the duration of the struggle, have our more recent strikes differed from it?

Three hundred thousand English workmen – twice the number of the military forces of the empire, and four times as many as won the battle of Waterloo – believing themselves to be mercilessly fleeced by a few hundred employers, volunteered to starve themselves and their families and involve thousands of their fellow-men in their misfortunes, accept charity and peacefully comport themselves, until such time as their immortal souls gave out or their masters discovered that it was no longer profitable to insist upon the additional rate of plunder.

It was not war. It was culpable, incomprehensible fatuity. Why, our solitary moulder, of whom I have just spoken, made more forcible protest over his trumpery twopence than did these well nigh half a million men over what presumably was to be a permanent purloining of five shillings a week off every man of them. No wonder we are termed a law-abiding people! But, please observe that the law is robbers' law, and we, the people who abide by it, have been described by Carlyle as mostly fools.

Extraordinary as is the conduct of workmen during a strike, it is eclipsed by their conduct afterwards. I have already rioted the peculiar circumstance that whenever you see a handsome church in the course of erection you can foretell that there will be a strike in the neighbourhood before many months are gone. Similarly, wherever a strike has taken place, you may be morally certain that the employer of labour who has proposed the hardest terms and has in all ways made himself most obnoxious to his workmen, will be elected Member of Parliament for the locality on the very first vacancy. I have gone elaborately into the statistics bearing on this point, and so remarkable are the coincidences of the two events that I have been forced to the conclusion that politicians deliberately reckon upon the fact, and arrange that whenever an employer wishes to get into Parliament he shall first win the esteem of the electorate by a vigorous course of wage reductions and lockouts. No matter how infuriated against their master workmen may be during a strike, a few months after it is over the majority of them appear to acquire quite an affection for him; and the more soundly they have been beaten, the more ardent becomes their attachment!

Turning meanwhile from the absurdity of the modes of strikes, and the manners of those who engage in them, let us look sharply for a moment into the ostensible purpose which they are designed to accomplish.

That strikes in nowise determine the right or wrong of the claims of the workers is evident not only from the circumstance that usually the lowest paid and most severely wrought trades have generally been the least successful, but from the far more important consideration that there exists, and can exist no means of deciding, under the present competitive commercial conditions, what is and what is not a fair wage. Even when the matter in dispute is brought to the test of the market value of the products, and when the profits of the capitalists have been reduced to the lowest percentage, we havs not reached any standard of value which will bear scrutiny. The market value of an article which has perhaps cost a great deal of labour may be very low, whereas that which has cost little or no labour may be very high. Goods are sometimes sold under the actual cost paid in wages for them, while at any other time they may be sold for ten, twenty, or thirty times their wage cost. A fisherman, for example, after bringing in a boatload of fish which has cost him a couple of days' labour in netting and hauling, may find that there is no demand whatever for his cargo, and may have to throw it away on the beach. A week later he brings in another load, and so great is the demand for his catch that he may sell it at double the price he had thought of asking for it. Of course, the irregularity in the quantity of fish produced is the chief cause of this great fluctuation in the price; but even were a fixed quantity of fish obtained every day from the sea, the competition of the buyers in the market would vary in intensity, and the wages of the fisherman would rise and fall in consequence.

The quantity of coal produced in this country does not, and certainly need not fluctuate much, yet the selling price and the wages paid to the miners fluctuate a great deal. For example[1], in the year 1890 the coal produced in Great Britain amounted to almost the same figure as in 1892 – 181,614,288 tons as against 181,786,871 tons – yet the selling price at the pit heads fell from £74,953,997 in 1890 to £66,050,451 in 1892, a difference of nearly 9 per cent. Again, during the period 1870-1874 there was an annual average export of 911,000 tons of railroad iron, and during the period 1885-1889 very nearly the same amount, viz., 915,000 tons. Yet from the former period to the latter, the price of the total had fallen from £9,420,000 to only £4,440,000. I am not here entering into the causes of the variation in the prices of products. I am merely noting the fact that they do vary even when the supply is approximately the same in quantity, and that consequently the selling price of commodities affords no equitable standard to which to appeal the question of wages. Even were masters content always to exact a uniform percentage of interest and profit, however low, workmen would find that the instability – under competition – of the market value of products would upon appeal justify frequent and considerable alterations in their wages. Nevertheless it is actually by this unstable and totally blind tribunal that masters in most instances profess to regulate the rates of wages; and it is by that, in the majority of instances, the success or failure of a strike is determined.

Of course, if the workers are sufficiently organised and determined they may, by prolonging a strike, occasionally succeed in compelling a rise of prices in the market, and thus make good for the moment their claim for an increase, or against a reduction, of pay. But this can only happen when the demand for the product is persistent, and when the market cannot be supplied from other districts or countries. Such favourable conditions are, however, of infrequent occurrence.

19

There are few articles of urgent and imperative need to the community, or any section of it, which are produced only in one locality, or in any one manufacturing area likely to be affected by a strike. Most of the primary and indispensable articles of consumption or use can be obtained in an emergency from widely separate districts or countries; and it rarely or never happens that in all these places there is any sharply simultaneous, defensive, or offensive action by the workers.

Footnote

1. Compare in this connection the dispute going on in Parliament even at this moment, between the miners and the Government, as to the necessity of a 14s. increase in the selling price of a ton of coal.

Chapter II

BUT if, on the one hand, the action of workmen in resorting to strikes is neither an accurate means of ascertaining what are fair wages, nor yet an effective means of securing them, neither on the other hand do the pleas usually put forward by employers, when resisting any increase, or insisting upon a reduction of wages, afford a truthful or sufficient justification of their conduct. These pleas may be summarised in the phrases, "Bad Trade," "Foreign Competition," "Low Prices," and "Diminished Profits."

Now, it is evident on the least thought about it that, even were the assertions true, as they often are not, workmen cannot be responsible for any of the circumstances implied in them.

It is not the working class, but the capitalist class that undertakes the organisation of industry and the control of the market for profitmaking. This is no accusative statement. It is the claim boastfully and triumphantly made on behalf of employers and capitalists generally, by themselves and their political apologists. And surely no more discreditable admission of their personal incompetence, or the unserviceableness of their functions could be desired, than this of their cwn, that they are unable to conduct the production and exchange of the country, with even such bare efficiency as will allow of their paying the paltry wages demanded by their workers, or of their obtaining for themselves the no more than petty profits which they allege their businesses afford. What object can there be in producing commodities at all, if neither those who make them, nor those who Organise those who make them, nor those even who sell them, can get a "living wage" out of the undertaking?

And if neither the workers can get wages, nor the employers profit, to whom does the enormous sum of our industrial profits go – a sum admittedly sufficient, even with our present recklessly wasteful methods of production, to richly supply all our material needs as a nation, and of which at present the workers, some four-fifths of the nation, only obtain one-third? Who are the clever knaves, and how do they get their greedy fingers in. who contrive so successfully to deplete the workers of the reward of their labour, and the astute employers of their tender percentages? And why don't the employers, the "captains of industry," the "statesmen of commerce," as they have, with prodigious flattery, been designated, seize hold of these wicked thieves and have them publicly arraigned for their crimes? Truly, if matters stand as said "captains" and "statesmen" protest upon all occasions of dispute with their workmen, they must either be imbeciles, and fit only to be confined in lunatic asylums, or themselves be the knaves, or the abettors of the knaves, in which case they should be stripped of their "captains'" uniforms, and deprived of their "statesmen's" seals, and sent to the places which they have prepared for their less dangerous, but more unfortunate professional brethren.

And if we inquire we shall find that our worst suspicions of the capitalists are confirmed at every turn. Their everyday actions, their mode of life, their places of abode, the company which they keep, and even their antecedents, all track them down as men of evil principles and unrighteous deeds.

Never a week passes but we find a list of wills in the newspapers in which fortunes of from £30,000 to £300,000, and occasionally £3,000,000, have been left by well-known or obscure capitalists, who have gone down into the pit, protesting with almost their last breath that their businesses did not pay, and that the workers must submit to a reduction of wages. Never a week passes but we read that some coalowner, ironmaster, manufacturer, shipowner, or railway shareholder, who has made himself notorious by resisting the demands of his workpeople, is about to build a new yacht, or a larger palace, purchase an additional shooting, or go away upon another prolonged tour in some interesting part of the world.

Again, too, in the reports of their financial successes

published in the commercial columns of our newspapers, we discover that however the profits of capitalists may shrink when held up to the gaze of the workers, they assume astounding proportions when laid for inspection before financial investors. When the Messrs. Coates, of Paisley, first converted their Thread Mills into a Limited Liability concern in 1898, they affirmed that they had been making an average annual profit of £480,000, and that they employed about 6,000 workpeople. That is to say, according to their own audited declaration, the firm was making a profit of not less than £78 a year, or 30s. a week off every one of the men, women and girls in its employment.

Hardly less astounding were the figures given by a firm of Tube manufacturers in the neighbourhood of Glasgow about the same time, in a prospectus issued for a similar purpose. By its own confession the firm was making a profit of more than £1 for itself, against every £1 paid out in wages to its workmen. Many colliery companies also admit making profits as high as from 15 to 35 per cent, on their nominal capital. [1]

It may be demurred that instances of this kind are exceptional, and that the great majority of employers obtain but meagre dividends upon their investments, not a few indeed failing to obtain any return at all.

But the objection only serves to exhibit more clearly the purely predatory character of our commercial system. Capitalists are not only purchasers of their workmen's labour, but sellers afterwards of what they have purchased. As buyers of labour they endeavour to get as much of it as possible, at the lowest cost in wages. As sellers to other capitalists, middlemen, agents, or consumers, they endeavour to give as little, and get as much in return as they possibly can. In this process of exchange between employers, middlemen, and consumers, it inevitably happens that one or other of them drives the most successful bargain. If the employer happens to be an incapable merchant of the goods which he has possessed himself of by his workmen's labour, he may have to sell at a price that allows him little or no profit on the transaction, in which case the purchaser, usually a middleman or broker of some description, pockets as extra gain what the employer has unwittingly let slip through his fingers. Thus, if I may present the matter in a familiar and perfectly accurate manner, the employer who has stolen so much value from his workmen fails, when disposing of it to the reseller, to get even a fair thieves' price for it. He is, however, none the less a knave, though he may be the greater fool that he has allowed another rascal to niggle him of his booty.

Perhaps, however, there may be workers who still cling to the peculiar notion that the capitalists and landlords, wno between them make up our employing classes today, do some really useful work, and that without them it would be impossible for industry to be carried on. Do they not, it may be asked, supply the capital, pay us our wages, and direct our labour wisely?

No! Employers do not supply workmen with either the capital they use, nor their wages, nor do they direct their labour wisely.

The landlords and capitalists simply hold possession of the land, which no one can claim to have produced, and the capital, which the labour and skill of the workmen have produced, and only allow the latter the further use of the land and capital on condition that tbey hand up to their employers all that they make, and are content to go on working for the small share they receive back in the form of wages. All the capital, viz., all the workshops, factories, machinery, railways, etc., which the capitalist class own, and all the houses, food, clothing, and everything else which workmen purchase with their wages, have been produced by the labour and skill of the workers of this and past generations. The capitalist class have obtained all the capital, which they now use to compel the workers to serve them, by the very same means as they now increase their store of it, that is, by unjust exchange, by paying the workers less in wages than the workers produce by their labour.

Moreover, they do not direct the workers' labour wisely. It must surely be admitted that there are only two questions with which a wise director of labour would trouble himself. He would first find out what the people needed, and secondly see to it that the workers who under him laboured to produce what was needed, had themselves their full life needs supplied – with all that that implies in comfort at their work, and the opportunity of leisure and pleasure outside of it – and that none of their labour force was wasted. Instead of this, today, the employers are exercising all their skill, their cunning, and, if you will, their anxiety and labour, in endeavouring to *sell* at a profit. That is, they will, firstly, only allow their land and capital to be used for the production of goods which other people have money to buy, and as the workers have little and the rich much, they prate of gluts in the market, and no work needing to be done, when the poor all around them are half-fed, half-clothed and half-sheltered. And secondly, whatever of time or diligence they do give to business is spent in fighting the other employers who desire to supply this cash demand, in obtaining orders for themselves which other employers would fain have secured.

Employers, therefore, do not assist in the production of wealth, they only manage or mismanage it with a view to getting as much for themselves, and as little for anybody else, as possible. Let me ask you, how, if the services of the capitalist class in any way add to the value of the products of labour, as all useful service must do, how is it that the reward of their service should be determined almost entirely by their cunning and craft in deceiving and over-reaching their neighbours? Why should they sometimes, almost without pretence of exertion at all, make large fortunes, and at other times, even with the utmost care and striving, fall out penniless? There are only two tenable suppositions. The one is that their services are dispensable and are, therefore, entitled to no due, constant, or ad valorem reward, in which case, whatever recompense capitalists obtain, is mere booty or spoliation gained by their preying upon the necessity or ignorance of those with whom they deal. The other is, that their services are indispensable and add to the value of the products of labour; in which case if they fail to obtain a due, constant, and *ad valorem* reward, as many, especially of the most active and just dealing, do fail, their failure must be the result of their being deprived of the value of their services unjustly by others of their own class. I say *of their own class* because the wages of workmen usually run at the same rate under employers who are unsuccessful, as under employers who are successful, and similarly, the prices paid by consumers are usually the same, irrespective of whether the goods have come from a firm that has made a profit or a loss in selling them. Whichever, therefore, of the two assumptions we proceed upon, we are forced to the conclusion that the existing capitalist-competitive system of production and exchange is fraught with grave injustice, and that as the employing classes cannot claim either to have furnished the workers with their capital or their wages, or to be directing their labour wisely, the whole system of their profit-making is based upon systematic theft.

Footnote

1. After-war figures make these statistics of profiteering read quite tamely. Since these paragraphs were written Messrs. Coates have declared a profit of over £19,000,000 for the five years of the war and topped this with a bonus of £7,300,000 capital to the shareholders from the reserve fund, in connection with a scheme which increased the company's capital from £10,000,000 to £20,000,000. The coal mines in the same period showed over £188,000,000 final net profits and interest accruing to coal owners, *after deducting the Coal Controller's Levy and the Excess Profits Duty!* The total capital sunk in the mines is about £135,000,000.

Chapter III

BUT while admitting the general effectiveness of strikes, and the dispensableness of the Capitalist classes, it may nevertheless be still urged that there is no prospect of the workers being released from the necessity of their position in the present or, maybe, for many generations to come, and that there is nothing for them but to make the best of it. They have to depend upon wages for their livelihood, and it is only by trade union organisation, and by resorting to strikes in extremities that they have improved their conditions in the past, and can hope to retain that improvement or to secure any further advance in the immediate future. Besides, it may be further urged, may not Trade Unions become stronger and accomplish more for the workers than they have yet done?

To take the last question first: What hope, think you, is there of Trade Unions becoming more powerful or more efficacious in the future? Already many of the trades have been as highly organised and equipped as they are ever likely to be, and they have had seasons of opportunity that will never recur again. Take the Lancashire Cotton Spinners, the Boilermakers' Society, the Amalgamated Engineers, and the Durham and Northumberland Miners' Association. These are large, rich and imposing unions. They are, or have been, splendidly organised, and have had all the power to yea or nay the terms of their employers that mere Trade Unions ever will have. Yet the members of those unions are still wage slaves, can still be thrust out of their jobs the moment their employers choose; their wages are still but little above the starvation rate paid to unorganised workmen, and their toil is as hard as it ever has been, even if their hours of labour be somewhat less than formerly. They cannot make bad trade good, they cannot, and would not dare if they could, prevent the introduction of wage-saving machinery; and even if it came to it they could not prevent their employers shutting their doors in their face never to open them again.

It may, however, be urged that although separate Trade Unions have failed, it is possible to form a national, and perhaps international, federation of Trade Unions, in the event of which the workers would have power to do as they chose. But do what? Merely regulate the conditions of employment? That would be a mountain in labour to bring forth a mouse, with a vengeance! But the proposition that a national, not to speak of an international, combination of the workers could be accomplished is untenable. It is almost inconceivable that all the workers in employment in every trade could be enrolled, and it certainly is inconceivable that these, even if enrolled, could support and carry with them all the unemployed, for whom there is no work now and never will be so long as the industries of the country are in the possession and worked for the profit of the Capitalist class. The further supposition that it is possible to combine all the workers of the world under existing national and economic conditions will not bear a moment's thought.

And about the masters. Already they are combining nationally and internationally, far faster than the workers can do or have any hope of doing. Suppose, if you will, that all the workers of this country were embraced in one vast federation of Trade Unions tomorrow, and all the capitalists were combined against them – what then? Truly the position would be as hopeless for the workers as it is in any instance today where it happens that all the men in one workshop go out on strike against one employer. If the workers were not resolved to take possession of the factories and the food supply; if they claimed only to be employed on better terms, then the masters would starve them out, or rather in, by the end of the first week.

If! But that "if" would never be. For did all the workers by any possibility ever come out on strike, and they realised what had really happened, *they never would go back again to work for employers*. The gigantic folly of such a, course would appal them. All the trappings of privilege with which their

28

superstition had invested their masters would instantly disappear. They would perceive that without their labour the richest idlers in the land would have to betake themselves out of the country, or become wretched vagabonds, grubbing scraps of offal from the streets, and that while the capitalists could not do without them, they could do admirably without the capitalists.

And it is precisely that fact which we as Socialists wish the workers to see now. We wish them to realise *beforehand* what would happen even if the workers and their masters were pitted against each other in one final nation-wide Trade Union conflict. Surely there is no workman but can form the picture in his mind's eye, and thus perceive that there would be only two alternatives before the workers in that improbable event. If they did no more than merely cease work they would speedily be in extremest destitution, while the richer capitalists might at a pinch get over to some foreign land, and there live comfortably till the workers begged them to come back and give them employment again! That the workers would be so insane as to starve themselves into submission in that manner is beyond belief. They would assuredly seize possession of the means of production and exchange, and never again allow their rich exploiters to touch a particle of their produce. In other words, they would cease to be mere strikers and become insurrectionists; they would no longer be Trade Unionists willing to work for wages, but Socialists determined to work co-operatively for the commonweal. And if that would be the upshot of a universal strike, could the same end not be achieved much better and more quickly without the disorganisation and disorder of a strike at all? And cannot the workmen living today, to whom the probability of there ever being a unanimous and simultaneous cessation of work must seem remote indeed, begin to act now?

While approving in the main what has been said, there are many who will exclaim:

"But have strikes done no good? What would be the use

of Trade Union combination at all unless strikes were resorted to on critical occasions? and, Have not Trade Unions raised wages and benefited the workers generally? Look at those industries in which there have been no Trade Unions and no strikes; compare the status of the disorganised with that of the organised workers!"

I am far from saying that nothing has been or that nothing can be done by strikes. Strikes have slightly increased wages, slightly reduced the hours, and slightly improved the general condition of the toilers, and may continue to do so in the future, but almost certainly to a lesser extent than formerly. Without the Trade Unions the workers would be a mere rabble of broken spirited and utterly degraded helots, and there would be little hope of their redemption. But what I wish to make very clear and convincing is, that by no strikes in the past have the workers dealt any effective blow at the system that persistently crushes them down; and that by no striking merely for wages or reduced hours can they in the future emancipate themselves.

If the workers do not wish to emancipate themselves, if they are content to remain mere raw material for the rentgrinding and profit-extracting processes of the rich, then strikes may perhaps compel their masters to adopt more refined methods of treatment; but if they wish to be no longer mere clay for the extraction of gold, but living men, rejoicing in the freedom of their lives and the fruits of their labour; then they must strike with their supremest strength, so as to splinter into fragments and dust the whole mechanism of the system that makes fragments and dust of themselves.

In the past the workers were ignorant, without combination, without political power. Trade Unions did almost magical work in giving them solidarity, strength, and political effectiveness. But they did not know – they could not know, for they were ignorant – nay, not they alone, but their masters also were ignorant, of the meaning of the struggle in which they found themselves involved. The Church had poured the poison of "original sin" and God's decrees into their minds, and they believed that everything was as it must be and only could be. All, therefore, that the Trade Unions hoped to be able to do was to lessen, if possible, the brutality of the power of the masters; and wherever Trade Unions have had a fair chance 'they have succeeded in their object. But today, the knowledge of the meaning of riches and poverty; the knowledge of the causes of the enslavement of the workers and the iniquity of the idleness and extravagance of the rich; the knowledge of the possibility of a new and nobler social and industrial life, has burst upon us with all the brightness and vivifying power of the summer sun; and are we now going to shut our eyes to the light, and grope about blindly in torment and fear as we did when in darkness? Shall we not rather see the error of our ways, the insufficiency of our deeds, and let our hearts, our thoughts, and our hands respond swiftly to the revelation that has come upon us?

When there were no highways in the land, travellers could not help losing their way sometimes, and even their lives. But what would you say of even the poor tramp who nowadays would refuse to see or avail himself of the great broad public paths, and preferred to wander up and down and round and round about in woods, bogs, and ditches, always coming back to the same place bruised, torn, and dripping with mud, under the impression that he was making great tracks ahead? What would you say of the man who would refuse to read books or newspapers, use the post-office or the steamboats or trains, who knew nothing about anything that was going on in the world except what he heard people talk of, and never went to see his sweetheart fifty miles up in the country, except when he had a week's holiday and could walk there? It is precisely the same with workmen who go out in the old-fashioned way on strike when they are a little more hard pressed than usual, and return to work when their bellies get empty, and never think of using the knowledge concerning their position and the political power of getting out of it, which is available at every hand. That workmen, until they have effectively used their knowledge and power, must still hold fast to their Trade Unions and come out as often, and stay out as long as possible, is of course obvious, just as it is obvious that where there is no highway across the country travellers must still find a path through woods and bogs and streams, and just as people must still accept information by word of mouth when they cannot get it otherwise, and tramp long distances on foot when they cannot obtain or pay for a train, or a steamboat, or a bicycle.

It is not the going out on strike when expedient that I am objecting to. It is to the fact that going out on strike should be expedient at all at this time of day; and that workmen, who ought to perceive the hopelessness of that means of progress, do absolutely nothing towards the plain, effective method of abolishing the conditions that render such a makeshift necessary.

Nor, surely, need I say that if strikes are wretched expedients, conciliation boards, sliding scales, and arbitrations are unspeakably worse. Folly, surely, could hardly go further than *these*. It is bad enough that workmen, because of their apathy and superstition, should have to submit to be robbed by the rich; but that they should form a joint tribunal, or make an agreeable arrangement with those who rob them, whereby the rate of robbery shall be mutually agreed upon, so that the rich shall be surer of their plunder and obtain it as pleasantly as possible, is a proposition that passes right out of the range of all rational contemplation. Let the rich, if they will, take like freebooters of old what they can, so long as they have the power, but make their taking as arduous and uncertain as possible. The easier and more agreeable their nefarious calling is made, the more tenaciously will they cling to it, and the more leisure they and their political hirelings will have to devote themselves to the recreation of obstructing the progress and corrupting the cause of the workers. The notion that although a man may give his master a day's labour of equal quantity and quality from week to week, yet the master may pay him a price that varies from week to week, may be admirably in accordance with the instincts of commerce, but hardly with those of good feeling and fair dealing. When a miner hews and draws three tons of coal today, he performs what is, presumably, a needful service to the community; if not, it is hardly his fault. When he does so three months hence his labour is presumably equally needful. And if his labour is equally needful then as now, why should he be paid a lower rate for it? No reason at all, save that his labour goes into a thieves' market. Certain it is that however the labour of a workman may vary from time to time in selling value, his own and his family's need for adequate sustenance and healthful conditions remains sufficiently constant and imperative.

Moreover, what has been said against strikes as a means of permanently uplifting the conditions of the working class applies with equal force against all remedial and palliative measures that do not make for the extinction of the present system of competitive capitalistic production. So long as the land and all the chief means of production are withheld from the workers, there is no hope either of any substantial or permanent improvement in the wages of the workers as a whole, or of any considerable section of them. For the only thing that a workman possesses, by which he can obtain the means of living, is his labour. Having no land and no material to labour upon, and no factories or machinery to assist him in his labour, and no means at his disposal for exchanging what he may produce by his labour, he is forced to sell his labour to those who possess these things, and who will only buy his labour at the lowest figure for which it can be had in the market. His labour, therefore, is merely a commodity – that is, a thing like cotton, iron, or bacon, the price of which today depends upon supply and demand. If there is much labour or much bacon wanted, and little to be had, the price goes up; if contrariwise, there is little demand for it and much to be had, the price goes down. It will thus be seen that the question of how far wages are likely to rise or fall in the market is very similar to that of how far the price of bacon is likely to rise or fall. If, therefore, we wish to ascertain what prospects there are of the workers being able to improve their position, either by strikes or any other expedient that still leaves them at the mercy of the market, we have simply to put the two following questions to ourselves:

- Is there any likelihood of the demand for labour increasing relative to the quantity of production?
- Is there any likelihood of the supply of labour diminishing again relative to the quantity of production?

To both of these questions a negative answer must be given ven in face of the great shortages temporarily produced by the war – unless, as I have already said, some direct legislative interference with competition and existing property rights takes place. Only a few of the reasons which justify this reply can be stated here, and necessarily very briefly. With respect to the first statement – that the demand for labour is not likely to increase, the following facts, which are persistent, may be cited:

1. The increasing use of machinery and improved processes of manufacture which enable manufacturers to dispense with the labour, especially of the skilled labour, of workmen.

2. The sub-division of the various branches of workmanship which likewise enables employers who manufacture on a large scale to do with less workmen, and here again especially of the skilled artisan class. Complementary to this may be included the extension of technical education, which by increasing the general efficiency of workmen's labour lessens the number of workmen required.

3. The loss of our foreign markets. Every day that passes brings other lands nearer an equality with our

own in productive capacity. At one time Britain manufactured so largely for foreign lands that it gained the appellation of the "workshop of the world." But now the world is fast becoming its own workshop; and the colonies and foreign nations are not only beginning to manufacture most things for themselves, but to compete with us in our own and other markets. Hopes have been entertained that there may at least be a temporary increase in production owing to the opening up of new markets in Africa and other "virgin" lands. The prospects of this occurring are, however, diminishing daily; and even if it did occur it would be of small importance to the wage-earners.

4. The formation of trusts, syndicates, and other combinations amongst capitalists, and co operative stores amongst working people, by means of which the waste of goods and labour of every description involved in competition is largely diminished, and thus also the need for workmen.

The second statement: That there is little likelihood of the supply of Labour diminishing, is confirmed by the following and many other circumstances:

1. The rapid increase of the population, especially of the wage-earning class, which no probable current of emigration, or the adoption of artificial or prudential restriction of the birthrate, is likely to materially lessen. With reference to the former, it may be noted that the advantage of starting in new lands is becoming less every day, and that the influx of immigrants from other countries into Britain is about as likely to augment the number of impoverished workers as the efflux of better-class artisans is to diminish it. Concerning the restriction of the birthrate, it need only be observed that in France,

where the population does not increase at all, poverty is almost as accentuated as at home.

2. The drifting of the rural population into the towns and manufacturing districts, a direct result of the present system of land monopoly.

3. The increasing opportunity for the employment of women and child labour through the introduction of machinery, new processes and sub-division of branches of manufacture, by which the need of strong and specially trained workmen is done away with.

4. The probable success of temperance legislation, which, if the hopes of its promoters are realised, will greatly increase the number of sober and industrious among existing competitors for work. To this may be added the proposed reduction or abolition of standing armies, and all other progressive measures likely to swell the ranks of the workers, or add to the efficiency of those already in the market.

Even, however, were it probable, notwithstanding all these apparently opposing circumstances, that labour would, from some cause or another, become "appreciated" in value, and wages rise somewhat, it is by no means certain that a rise in wages would be of any real advantage to the workers. For, paradoxical as it may sound, it is very doubtful if under the existing system of capitalistic production an increase in the nominal amount of wages enables the working class to obtain a corresponding increase in their share of the world's goods. For, mark you, the monopoly of land and capital is antecedent to competition, and capitalists only compete with a view to profit-making. When competition brings down the price of goods towards the point where profits vanish, competition automatically diminishes or ceases altogether. Usually when employers in a given trade are compelled to increase wages, they recoup themselves by increasing the price of what they sell, or by contriving to do with less wage-paid labour.

The advance in wages comes, therefore, not out of the pockets of the employers, but chiefly out of the pockets of the general community of workers. Even were wages increased all round the price of commodities would probably be increased all round also, and the seeming advantage to the workers prove illusory. If, for example, the average wage were raised from 20/– to 25/– the workers would find that they could purchase little if anything more with 25/– than they formerly did with 20/–. The accuracy of this statement is borne out by a comparison of the wages paid in various lands. Roughly speaking, the nominal rate of artisans' wages in America is twice as high as in Britain, and in Britain twice as high as in Germany. Nobody, however, who is acquainted with the condition of the working class in these countries, would affirm that workmen in America are twice better off than workmen in Britain, and four times better off than workmen in Germany. The cost of living in America and England is higher than in Germany proportionately, or nearly so, to the higher wages. As a matter of fact the average economic conditions of the artisan class, if accurately investigated, are much the same in all capitalist countries, irrespective of what the rate of wages may be. [1]

This unfavourable forecast of the future of Labour, proceeds, I must again repeat, on the assumption that the present unrestrained "free sale" of labour in the market shall not be interfered with by protective legislation, or by State or Municipal undertakings conducted on Socialist principles without regard to profit-making. In other words, it proceeds upon the supposition that the fight between the owners of the instruments of production and the workers shall be fought on the old field of "freedom of contract" with the old Trade Union weapons, and with no force of the State to back up the workers in their contest. Such a supposition is, you will readily perceive, a very unwarranted one. Already the State has interfered with the so-called rights of property and the liberty of employers to deal exactly as they choose with their wage-slaves, and at the present moment are there not demands on all hands for further intervention on behalf of the workers? Yes, but pray observe what that admission signifies. It implies, and that most accurately too, that the workers have been unable to sustain themselves in their struggle with the capitalist classes, and *have already had to appeal for help to the common conscience of the community.* It implies that Trade Unions, with all their weapons of offence and defence, have failed in the contest, and that *the State, in its capacity as the preserver (however inadequately) of the commonweal, has had to take up the workers' cause.* It implies that the people as a community cannot allow its well-being to be jeopardised, or the fate of its members decided by an unseemly and continual squabble between starving workmen and rich employers, and that whenever a peace bargain is made that is obviously detrimental to the prosperity of the people it must be set aside.

Thus it seems clearly proven that not only have Trade Union conflicts been unsuccessful in destroying the oppression and preventing the exploitation of labour in the past, but that in the future they are not likely, unaided, even to maintain what little ground of vantage they have gained. On the other hand, it is equally evident that whatever substantial and permanent modification of the merciless power of capitalism has taken place has been accomplished by the sentiment and action of the community as such, and that to this community or State effort we must look for all desirable and attainable improvement in the lot of the working class in the future.

Footnote

1. The soundness of this reasoning has been proved so clearly by the after-war relations between wages and prices, or "the cost of living," that even the dullest thinker will today admit its truth.

Chapter IV

MANIFESTLY, then, the problem now before the workers is not how they can best strive by combination, and if need be by strikes, to compel their masters to give them an increase of wages or a reduction of hours; but rather how they can soonest and best obtain possession of all the wealth, and avail themselves of all the leisure which their own industry entitles them to. And it is surely equally clear that they never can gain these except by undoing the power of their masters altogether, by themselves regaining possession of the land and other instruments of industry which have been cultivated or created by their own and their forefathers' intelligence and toil.

In other words, the workers must strike, if they would strike with enduring results, not against the effects of monopoly, hut against monopoly itself; not against the conditions which their masters impose upon them, but against the power of their masters to impose conditions at all.

And how can this be done? Only by, it is obvious, exercising their sovereignty as the PEOPLE, and declaring void all the legal claims and customs by which their masters hold possession of their wealth and dominion over the workers' lives. By, in fact, asserting their own just right and actual might over the spurious rights and fictitious might of those who have appropriated the land and capital of the country. For it is only in the name of and by the assumed consent of the people that their intolerable privileges are preserved by the legal statutes and the power of the military and police; and so soon as the people choose, they can in their own name, and of their own will, revoke these statutes; and, if need be, which is not likely, call upcn the military and police to give effect to their decrees, or, what would be more effectual, disband these discredited agents of law and order altogether.

Thus we see that it is by combining and striking

39

politically as the People against the system of monopoly itself, rather than by combining and striking as wage slaves against the mere operations of the system, that the freedom and wealth of the working classes can be regained. But the question comes – how can we strike politically? How can we dislodge the rich people from all the places of council and administration which they occupy in the land without at the same time producing great disturbances, probably bloodshed, and raaybe landing ourselves in a worse predicament than before? Give us, it may be asked, some practical proposal, something that we can set about doing now, not something which perhaps we ought to do, but which we cannot do all of a heap until may be many generations to come. Very good. Butastounding as it may seem at first sight, the most practical, the simplest, and the most equitable proposal that can be made is for us to do it now and completely when we are at it! Half truths are usually worse than whole lies; and half, quarter, and hundredth part measures of justice are, to say the least of it, generally little better than no justice at all. One of the greatest of the seeming justifications of political conservatism is the fact that so many half or quarter measures of reform have been tried in place of whole ones, and have, not only failed to accomplish their object, but have made matters worse than before. Half loaves may be better than no bread, but half an oven cannot bake them. It isn't political loaves we want. It is access to the ovens. If we don't have access to the ovens, and bake our bread ourselves, it will be sorry half loaves that we will get, more likely half bricks!

In many countries now, insurrectionary methods have been resorted to by strikers without visible success save as a costly political demonstration. Violent rebellion on the part of a portion of the workers is a hopeless expedient, so long as they must count upon the opposition of the forces of the State, backed up by the political support of the majority of the people, including the majority of the working class. When the insurrectionists form or can hope by any manifestation of their resolution, to form the majority, they can then also form the

State, and physical rebellion will be unnecessary. However heroic an appeal to guns, swords, and dynamite – the weapons of imperial and religious barbarism – may sound, it nevertheless resolves itself eventually into a prosaic counting of noses; and noses may as well be counted peacefully and accurately at the ballot box, as turbulently and inaccurately amid the dripping uf blood and splashing of brains. Whatever is established by the sword has usually to be secured by chains, you cannot displace one force without replacing it by another. When the workers are opposed by physical force, the workers – certainly the Rebel section – will not hesitate to resort to it also: but meanwhile it is not the force of the landlords and capitalists, nor of their armies nor police, that keeps the workers in servitude or keeps back Socialism, but the ignorance and apathy and the force of the workers themselves. The Social Revolution is not the despotism of a class but the co-operation of the people.

Hitherto the House of Commons, Municipal Councils, School Boards and all other administrative bodies which derive their authority and their funds from the people, of which the workers form the egregious majority, have been mainly, and often exclusively, composed of their masters – the landlords, employers of labour, rich merchants, and their legal abettors; and the people have placed them there. They have voted for them because they are so much accustomed to doing as they are bid in their factories and workshops that they follow their masters' call even into the polling booth!

Trade Unionists feel deeply incensed when their fellow workmen "blackleg" during a strike; but a man may blackleg against Labour in the ballot-box as well as in the workshop. And the Trade Unionist who votes for an employer of labour, or a landlord, or for any other than an avowed Socialist, is guilty of a far mote hurtful and disgusting form of blacklegging than is the poor unemployed workman who hastens to take the job of a man on strike.

If a fraction of the money spent unavailingly on strikes

were devoted to direct political effort, within the next five years the workers could turn every landlord and capitalist out of every legislative and administrative body in the land and put in Socialist delegates instead. They could thus, without confusion and without fear, become themselves the possessors of their own land, and all the stores, factories, machinery, mines, railways, ships, and other useful things which have been created by their own and their fathers' labour and skill, and use them in the interest of the whole community. They could arrange and manage their own industries just as they manage their own National Postal and Educational Systems today, their various Municipal undertakings, their co-operative stores, their trade and friendly societies, etc., only with this difference, that the wealth produced would be for the common advantage of all who helped in its production or otherwise served the community, and not chiefly for the advantage of particular classes or highly-paid officials. They could make sure that everyone had an opportunity of assisting in the production of wealth, and that everyone had an opportunity of enjoying it. The old, the sick, the physically or mentally unfit would be as tenderly cared for as our own children, and neither hardship for today nor anxiety for tomorrow would mar the excellence of our lives.

The realisation of such a state of society would surely be worth striving, worth striking for. And when we bear in mind that it could be done in the course of a year or two, by availing ourselves of our rights and performing our public duties as citizens, surely we ought to be ashamed of our apathy, iand of the miserable makeshift of strikes, which has served as the utmost manifestation of our manhood's courage and intelligence for so long.